# Massachusetts

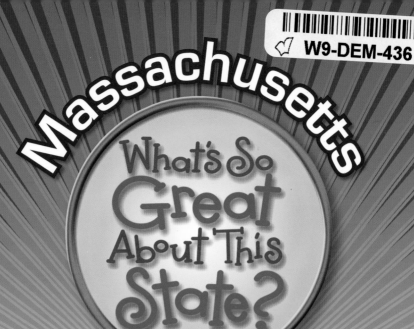

## What's So Great About This State?

There is a lot to see and celebrate...just take a look!

## CONTENTS

Land . . . . . . . . . . . . . . . . . . . . . . . . . . . . . . . .pages 2–9
History. . . . . . . . . . . . . . . . . . . . . . . . . . . . . . . .pages 10–17
People . . . . . . . . . . . . . . . . . . . . . . . . . . . . . . . .pages 18–25
And a Lot More Stuff! . . . . . . . . . . . . . . . . . .pages 26–31

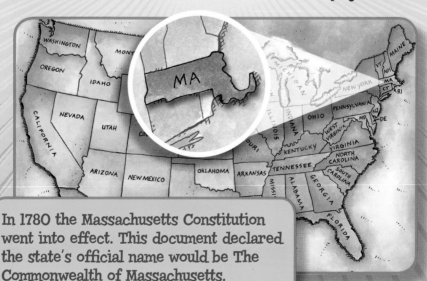

In 1780 the Massachusetts Constitution went into effect. This document declared the state's official name would be The Commonwealth of Massachusetts.

# Well, how about... the land!

## From the Eastern Shores...

Massachusetts is one of six states that form the New England region of the United States. (Maine, New Hampshire, Vermont, Rhode Island, and Connecticut are the other five states.)

Around 20,000 years ago, glaciers still covered the land. As the climate warmed, the glaciers slowly retreated leaving interesting landforms and a roller coaster of elevations, or land heights.

At sea level, natural harbors create safe ports along the eastern coastline. Peninsulas, such as Cape Ann and Cape Cod, jut out into the water. Wind and waves surround both big and small offshore islands.

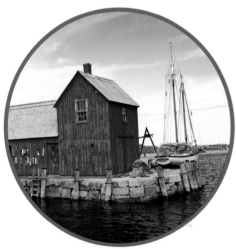

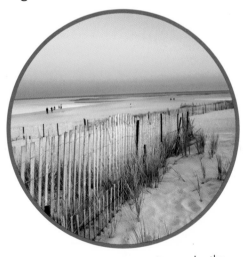

This fishing shack in Rockport, a village on Cape Ann, has been used in so many photos and paintings that it is now famously called Motif No. 1.

Hundreds of miles of shoreline make the Cape Cod beaches very popular vacation spots in summer.

# ...to the Western Hills

As you move away from the coast and further inland, the land begins to rise into the hills and mountains of the Eastern Upland region. But not for long! Elevations fall into the Connecticut River Valley when you reach the middle of the state.

The ride doesn't stop there. Western "Mass" is home to the Berkshire Hills and Mount Greylock, which—at 3,491 feet—is the highest point in the state.

It's quite an adventure to explore the land across Massachusetts. Turn the page to see just some of the interesting places you can visit throughout the state!

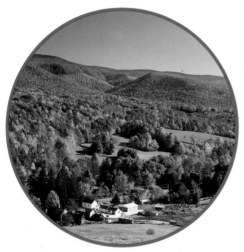

Western "Mass" is home to the Berkshire Hills, which blaze with color in the fall.

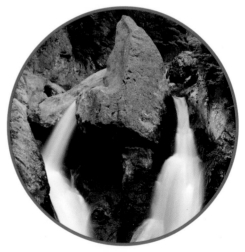

In the southwestern corner of the state, a huge boulder splits the water into two sections at Bash Bish Falls.

A beautiful sunset reflects off the water at Martha's Vineyard.

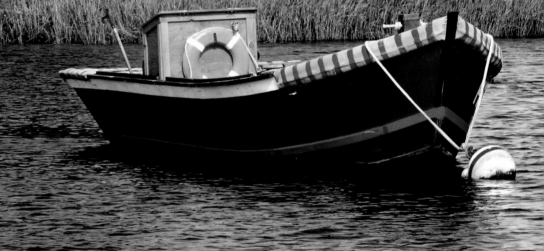

# The Coastal Lowland

COASTAL LOWLAND

A small fishing boat floats in marshy waters on Cape Cod.

The Coastal Lowland region covers one third of the state and extends all the way to the Atlantic Ocean. This region also includes islands off the coast, such as Plum Island, the Elizabeth Islands, Nantucket, and Martha's Vineyard.

## What's so special about the Coastal Lowland region?

Even though the land is mostly low-lying, there are many interesting things to see. Small oval-shape hills, or drumlins, are the calling cards of ancient glaciers in some parts of this region. Marshes, small lakes, and ponds also dot the landscape. Beautiful beaches and natural harbors are common sights along the coast.

## ...and there's more!

The Cape Ann peninsula along the northern coastline requires six lighthouses to keep ships safe from its rocky shores. Along the southern coastline, huge sand dunes at the Cape Cod National Seashore offer a lookout for ocean-going whales.

Plum Island is one of the barrier islands along the state's northern shore. It lies close to the mainland and shields coastal beaches from wind and ocean waves. But Massachusett's most famous islands—Martha's Vineyard and Nantucket—sit farther away from the mainland off the southern coast of the state.

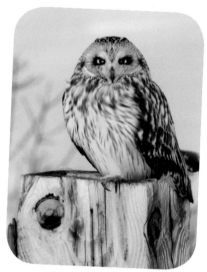

This owl is not bothered by winter snow along the northern coast of the state.

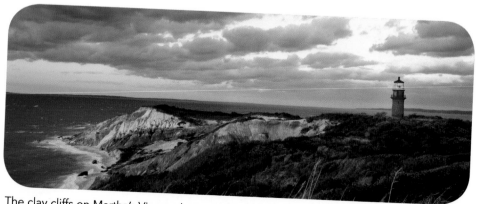

The clay cliffs on Martha's Vineyard are constantly pounded by ocean waves.

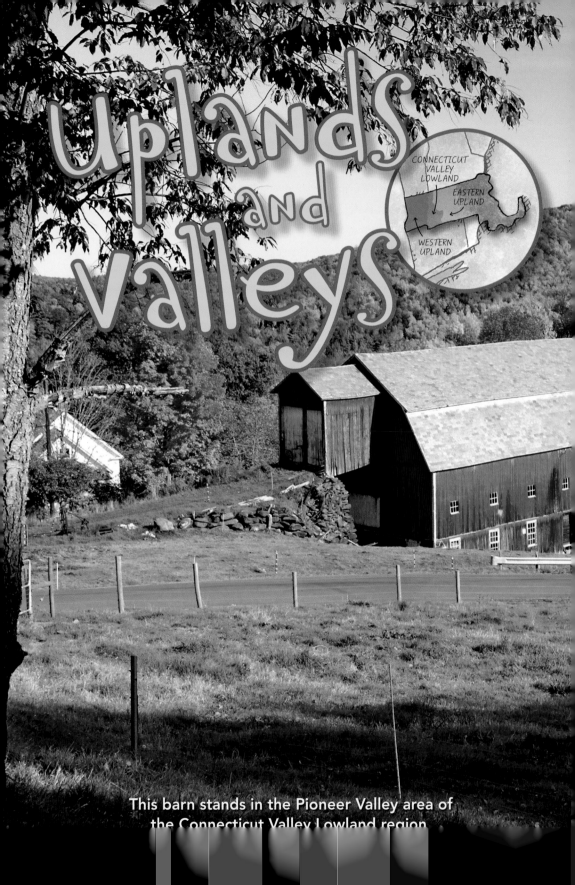

# Uplands and Valleys

CONNECTICUT VALLEY LOWLAND

EASTERN UPLAND

WESTERN UPLAND

This barn stands in the Pioneer Valley area of the Connecticut Valley Lowland region.

Just west of the Coastal Lowland, the Eastern Upland begins. The land rises up to 1,000 feet above sea level in this area. Skiers and hikers love the trails and beautiful views of the hills and mountains in this region.

## Then the land takes a dip!

Just west of the Eastern Upland region, the land begins to slope down to the Connecticut Valley Lowland region. The Connecticut River flows through the valley. Some of the best soil in the state can be found in this region so it's a good place for farmers to grow fruit and corn and raise livestock.

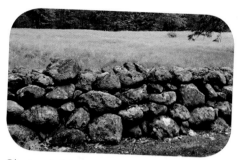

Glaciers left loads of rocky debris on Massachusetts land so it's common to see walls and fences fashioned from stones rather than wood.

## Don't forget the Western Upland!

Continue into the Western Upland region and the land begins to rise again. The Berkshire Hills are covered in thick forests. Freshwater streams provide homes for fish, muskrat, and beaver.

Just west of the Berkshire Hills (before you get to the far western Taconic Mountains) lies the Berkshire Valley. This narrow valley —only ten miles at its widest—runs the whole length of the state and is a prime location for grazing cows and dairy farms.

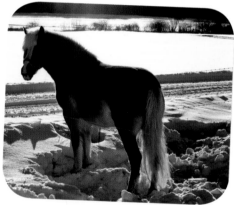

Cows aren't the only critters raised in western Massachusetts, as this snow-covered horse farm shows!

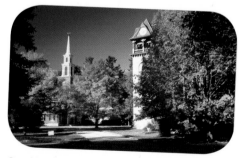

Stockbridge is one of the many beautiful towns in the Berkshire Hills of western Massachusetts.

# Ponds, Lakes, and Rivers

New England's longest river, the Connecticut River, flows north to south through Massachusetts.

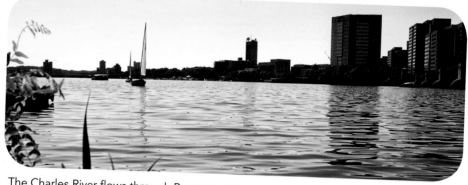

The Charles River flows through Boston on its way to the Atlantic Ocean.

Massachusetts has thousands of miles of rivers and streams flowing throughout the state. Several major rivers include the Charles, the Connecticut, the Merrimack, and the Housatonic. But that's not the end of the water resources. The state has more than three thousand lakes and ponds—some of which are kettle ponds.

## What's a kettle pond?

Glaciers at work again! As huge chunks of ice retreated from the land ten to twenty thousand years ago, they carved holes in the land's surface, forming many of the state's lakes and ponds. However, kettle ponds were created just a little differently. They formed when buried blocks of ice melted, causing the sand and gravel above them to collapse into a hole.

Walden Pond, made famous through the writings of Henry David Thoreau, is probably the most famous kettle pond in Massachusetts.

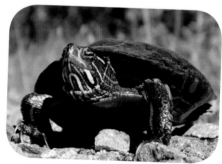

## Why are lakes, rivers, and ponds so special?

That's an easy one! These water resources provide recreation, transportation, food, and habitats. Most important, they supply

Lots of different wildlife, including this painted turtle, live at Walden Pond State Reservation.

drinking water. In fact, the largest lake in Massachusetts is an artificial lake called the Quabbin Reservoir. It was built in the 1930s to help meet the freshwater needs of the capital city of Boston and surrounding communities.

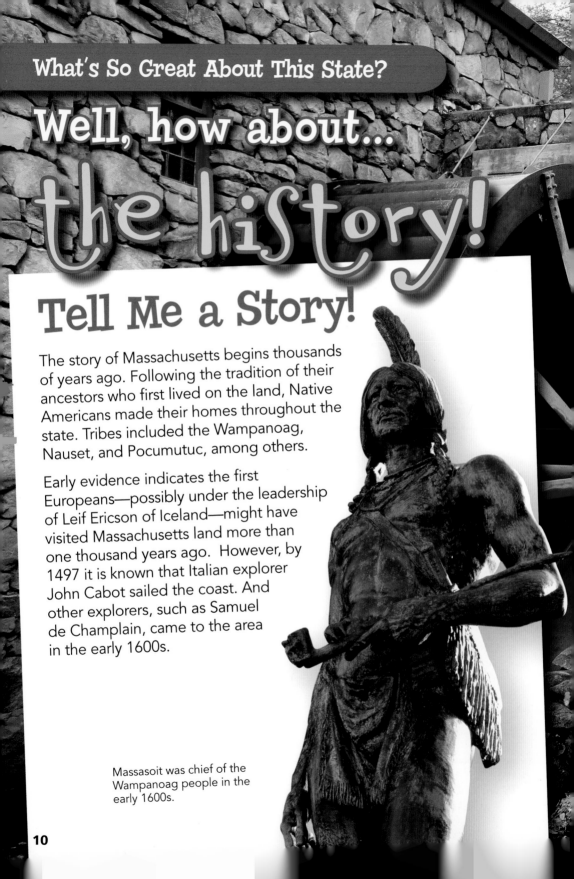

# Well, how about...

# the history!

## Tell Me a Story!

The story of Massachusetts begins thousands of years ago. Following the tradition of their ancestors who first lived on the land, Native Americans made their homes throughout the state. Tribes included the Wampanoag, Nauset, and Pocumutuc, among others.

Early evidence indicates the first Europeans—possibly under the leadership of Leif Ericson of Iceland—might have visited Massachusetts land more than one thousand years ago. However, by 1497 it is known that Italian explorer John Cabot sailed the coast. And other explorers, such as Samuel de Champlain, came to the area in the early 1600s.

Massasoit was chief of the Wampanoag people in the early 1600s.

# ...The Story Continues

The first European settlers who came with their families to stay arrived in 1620, from England. About one hundred passengers from the Mayflower came ashore at what is now called Plymouth. Many of the passengers were Church of England Separatists—a group who became known as the Pilgrims. In 1630, a large wave of people from a different religious group, called the Puritans, arrived from England to settle as part of the Massachusetts Bay Colony.

Eventually, Massachusetts became home to many other people. Their footprints are stamped into the soul of Massachusetts history. You can see evidence of this all over the state!

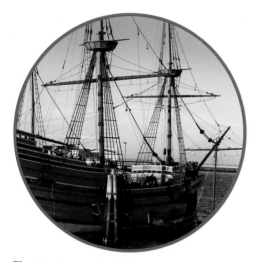

The Mayflower II at Plimoth Plantation is a replica, or copy, of the small wooden ship that crossed the Atlantic Ocean in 1620. Imagine what it would've been like to travel with farm animals and one hundred other people over the open ocean—for two months!

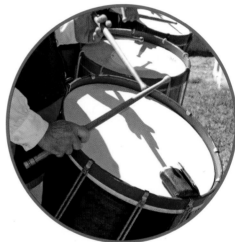

The first battles of the American Revolutionary War were fought in Lexington and Concord in April of 1775. (This is when Paul Revere made his famous ride to warn that the British were coming.)

The Wayside Inn Grist Mill in Sudbury uses water power to grind wheat into flour.

# MONUMENTS

Bronze statues in Springfield, Massachusetts, honor Dr. Seuss and some characters from his books.

Monuments, memorials, and historic sites honor special people or events. The Dr. Seuss National Memorial in Springfield honors hometown author Theodor Seuss Geisel—better known as Dr. Seuss!

## Why are Massachusetts monuments so special?

That's an easy one! Many special people helped build the state of Massachusetts. Some, like politicians and presidents, were famous when they lived. Others became better known over time. Paul Revere is a good example! This hero of the American Revolution rode on horseback throughout the night to warn people of a British attack. His alert helped save John Hancock and Samuel Adams from capture. Statues honor Revere's bravery, and Henry Wadsworth Longfellow spread his fame by paying tribute to Revere's famous midnight ride in a well-loved poem.

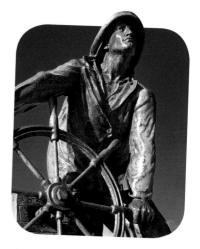

The "Man at the Wheel" statue in Gloucester is dedicated to fishermen who have been lost at sea.

## What kind of monuments can I see in Massachusetts?

There are many different kinds. From statues to bridges, almost every town has found some way to honor a historic person or event. Even street signs often show the name of someone special.

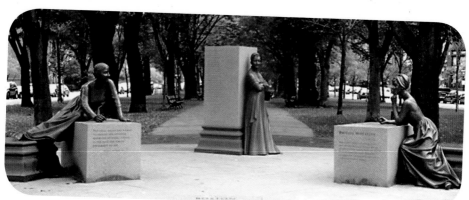

The Boston Women's Memorial on the Commonwealth Avenue Mall honors three women who made important contributions to the history of Massachusetts—Abigail Adams, Lucy Stone, and Phyllis Wheatley. The sculptor, Meredith Bergmann, purposely shows the women using their pedestals…not standing on them!

# MuSEuMS

The USS *Constitution* was first commissioned in 1797 and it is still part of the U.S. Navy fleet.

Museums tell you about history in such interesting ways! At the USS Constitution Museum in Boston you can learn about the three-masted Navy vessel that is nicknamed "Old Ironsides." You can also learn what the life of a sailor was like in the early 1800s—from furling sails to scrubbing the decks.

## Why are the museums in Massachusetts so special?

Museums tell many different stories. The Norman Rockwell Museum in Stockbridge has the largest collection of Rockwell paintings in the world. This famous American artist painted scenes showing the daily life of people—including many who lived near him in the Massachusetts Berkshire region.

## What can I see in a museum?

An easier question to answer might be "What can't I see in a museum?" Of course, different museums have different artifacts, or objects. The Museum of Fine Arts in Boston has about 400,000 pieces of art, ranging from Egyptian mummies to Native American pottery. The Spellman Museum of Stamps and Postal History in Weston holds more than two million artifacts that give a historical view of the country and promote the hobby of stamp collecting.

This stamp celebrated the state of Massachusetts—back when postage was only 37 cents!

GREETINGS FROM MASSACHUSETTS

USA 37

2002

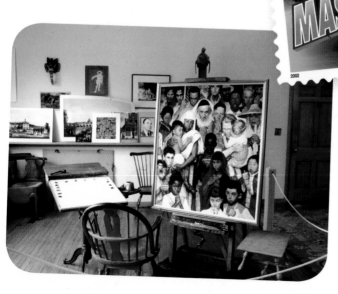

At the Norman Rockwell Museum you can see the studio where the artist worked. The painting shown here, called *The Golden Rule*, was a famous *Saturday Evening Post* magazine cover in 1961.

# Forts

Fort Independence is on Castle Island in the Boston Harbor.

The first fort on Castle Island was built by the British. However, the fort was given its current name—Fort Independence—after Americans had won independence in the Revolutionary War. The present-day fort (the eighth one built on the site) is a state park.

## Why are forts special? (...and what is a fort, anyway?)

A fort is a defensive structure built for troops. Forts played important roles in the struggle for independence in the early history of our country.

The inside of a fort was often a self-contained community. That's because soldiers often had to stay inside the fort during long attacks. A fort had barracks—places for soldiers to sleep—as well as kitchens for water and food supplies. Forts even had repair shops to keep battle equipment in top shape.

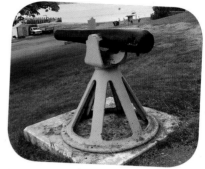

## What can I see if I visit a fort?

Some forts show you what life was like long ago. You can see artifacts, including cannons and other weapons soldiers used. Other forts are now peaceful parks where you can walk and sightsee.

A cannon used in the Civil War still stands at Fort Warren on George's Island, which is now part of the Boston Harbor Islands National Recreation Area.

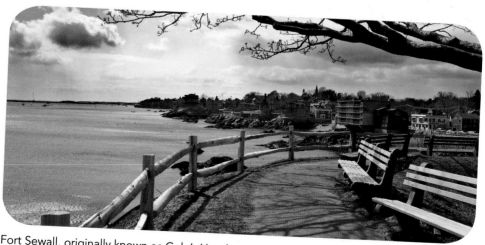

Fort Sewall, originally known as Gale's Head, was renamed to honor Marblehead native and Massachusetts Supreme Court Justice Samuel Sewall. The fort is now a park with beautiful views of the Marblehead Harbor.

# Well, how about...
# the people!

## Enjoying the Outdoors

More than six and a half million people call Massachusetts home. As hearty New Englanders, Bay Staters know that harsh winter weather sometimes brings challenges. However, most have a deep respect for the land and share a love of the outdoors.

With four distinct seasons, people in Massachusetts can enjoy different activities all year long. Skiing in the winter, rafting in the spring, swimming and hiking in the summer—the list of things that Bay Staters enjoy goes on and on!

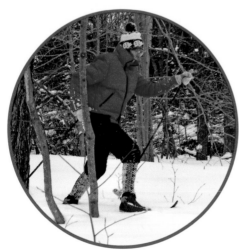

Cross-country skiing provides a winter workout in the Berkshire area of western Massachusetts.

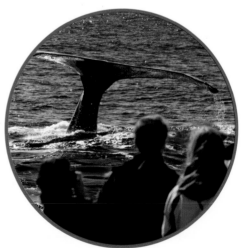

Whale watching is popular off the coast of Massachusetts from spring through fall.

# Sharing Traditions

Massachusetts is rich in traditions. You can find evidence of this all over the state. Re-creations of distant battles honor brave soldiers. Interesting festivals showcase skills (from quilting to repairing fishnets) that have been passed from one generation to the next.

Cooking is another way to pass on traditions. Portuguese, Italian, Irish—the tasty dishes served on tables throughout the state come from many different cultures. Locally grown food, like cranberries and apples, are used in many recipes. Freshly caught oysters, clams, cod, and lobsters also add to the tasty mix.

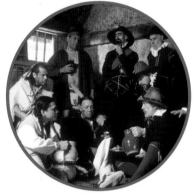

You can learn 17th-century English at Plimoth Plantation. Instead of saying "Congratulations," the English colonists might have said "Huzzah!"

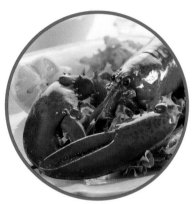

Cracking open a freshly cooked lobster requires practice…and a large bib!

A rocky shore at the Annisquam Lighthouse in Gloucester.

# Protecting

A yellow warbler perches on a branch at the Parker River National Wildlife Preserve in Newburyport.

The Parker River National Wildlife Preserve was originally opened to provide feeding, resting, and nesting habitats for migratory birds. Today, the refuge's mission is even greater as it helps protect threatened and endangered species in the state.

## Why is it important to protect the natural resources of Massachusetts?

Although the state of Massachusetts is not very large, it still has plenty of different environments within its borders. All these different environments mean lots of different plants and animals live throughout the state. In technical terms, Massachusetts has great biodiversity. This biodiversity is important to protect because it keeps the environments balanced and healthy.

## What kinds of organizations protect these resources?

Protecting all of Massachusetts's natural resources is a full-time job for many people! State organizations such as the Massachusetts Department of Conservation and Recreation and the Massachusetts Department of Environmental Protection work to manage, protect, and preserve the state's natural resources and heritage. Of course, there are many other private groups at work, too, such as the Massachusetts Audubon Society and the Rachel Carson Council.

## And don't forget...

You can make a difference, too! It's called "environmental stewardship"—and it means you are willing to take personal responsibility to help protect Massachusetts's natural resources.

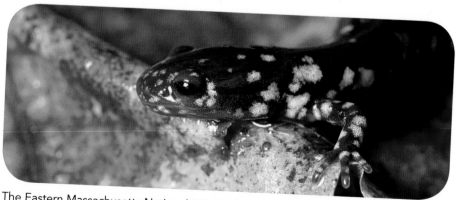

The Eastern Massachusetts National Wildlife Refuge Complex has a Citizens Science Program. So if you see a rare animal on refuge land, like this blue-spotted salamander, the staff wants you to report it. They will then add the sighting to their records, which helps their conservation efforts.

# Creating Jobs

Cranberries are harvested in the bogs
of southeastern Massachusetts.

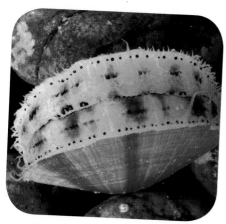

New Bedford is famous for its yearly harvest of sea scallops.

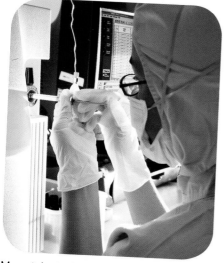

Many jobs in the state require research skills.

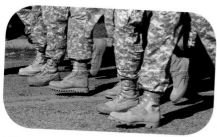

Military training is hard work!

Some jobs have been done in Massachusetts for a long time. Farming is one of them. Fishing along the Atlantic coast is another. Other jobs—in research and technology—are newer to the state.

## What other kinds of work do people do throughout the state?

Manufacturing, or making things, is common. Years ago, textile manufacturing (basically, making cloth) was very big. Today, however, computer equipment and plastic products are more likely to be produced.

Many people also now work in the finance industry. Health care and education are also in demand.

Technology service positions require computer programmers and engineers. The tourist industry also needs service providers. It takes a lot of workers to help people sightsee, eat, and relax!

## Don't forget the military!

The Air Force, Army, Marine Corps, Navy, and Coast Guard can all be found in the state. The people of Massachusetts have great respect for all the brave men and women who serve our country.

# Celebrating

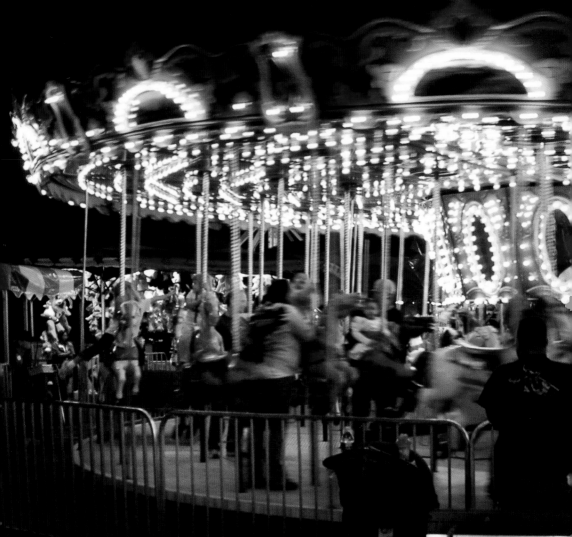

The carousel ride is great fun at the Big E in West Springfield.

The people of Massachusetts really know how to have fun! West Springfield is home to the largest fair in New England—the Eastern States Exposition. Called the Big E, it attracts more than a million people each year to enjoy everything from rides and music to animal exhibits and food.

## Why are Massachusetts festivals and celebrations special?

Celebrations and festivals bring people together. From cooking and farming to arts and entertainment, special events across the state celebrate the people of Massachusetts and their talents.

## What kinds of celebrations are held in Massachusetts?

Too many to count! But one thing is for sure. You can find a festival or celebration for just about anything you want to do.

Do you like pig races? You can cheer for your favorite porker at the Martha's Vineyard Agricultural Fair.

Or maybe you'd like to sample some interesting new types of food? The Lowell Folk Festival celebrates food and music from all over the world.

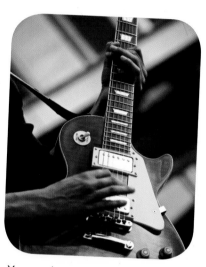

You can hear great music at the Salem Jazz and Soul Festival.

## ... and don't forget the skillet toss!

Skillet tossing is a popular contest for both men and women at the Festival of the Hills in Conway. How does it work? Just like it sounds! Whoever tosses a heavy skillet the farthest wins!

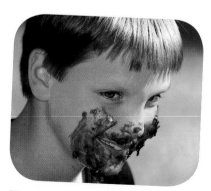

Pie-eating contests—like the kind they have at the Truro Agricultural Fair—can produce results like this!

# Birds
## and
# Words

What do all the people of Massachusetts have in common?
These symbols represent the state's shared history and natural resources.

## State Tree
### American Elm

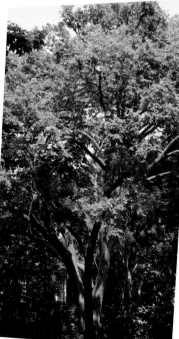

## State Bird
### Black-capped Chickadee

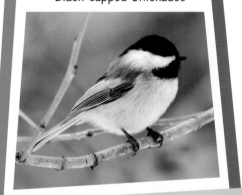

## State Flower
### Mayflower

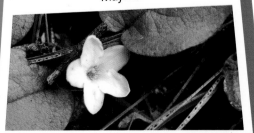

# State Berry
Cranberry

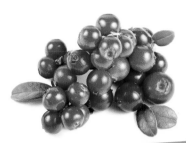

# State Flag

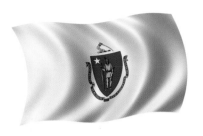

# State Reptile
Garter Snake

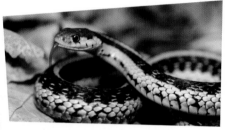

# State Game Bird
Wild Turkey

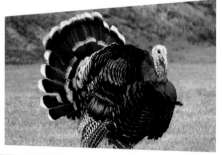

# State Horse
Morgan

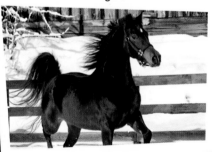

# State Muffin
Corn Muffin

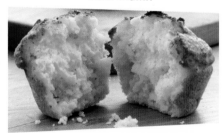

# Want More?

**Statehood**—February 6, 1788
**State Capital**—Boston
**State Nickname**—The Bay State
**State Song**—"All Hail to Massachusetts"
**State Sport**—Basketball

**State Beverage**—Cranberry Juice
**State Fish**—Cod
**State Mammal**—Right Whale
**State Dance**—Square Dance
**State Cookie**—Chocolate Chip

# More Fun Facts

## More

Here's some more interesting stuff about Massachusetts.

## A Tribal Name

Massachusetts takes its name from the Massachusett tribe of Native Americans, who lived south of Boston in the Great Blue Hill area.

## A Presidential County

Four U.S. presidents were born in **Norfolk County**: John Adams, John Quincy Adams, John Fitzgerald Kennedy, and George Herbert Walker Bush.

## A Whale of a Tale

In 1841 Herman Melville sailed out of **New Bedford** on a whaling ship. Years later, while living in **Pittsfield**, he wrote his most famous book, called *Moby-Dick*. However, the book was not considered a huge success until many years after his death.

## An Apple a Day

Johnny Appleseed (whose real name was John Chapman) was born in **Leominster** in 1774.

## A Yearly Tea Party

The reenactment of the Boston Tea Party takes place at the Old South Meeting House in Boston each year.

## A Primary Park

Boston Common (in **Boston**, of course!) is the oldest public park in the country. It was established in 1634.

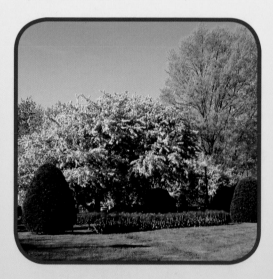

## How Sweet It Is

The fig newton was named after the city of **Newton**.

## "Southie" Irish Spirit

St. Patrick's Day is a popular celebration in Massachusetts. The **South Boston** St. Patrick's Day Parade has been a tradition since 1901.

## Be Happy!
Harvey Ball of **Worcester** designed the world-famous Smiley face.

## The Belle of Amherst
Emily Dickinson wrote nearly 1,800 poems. But fewer than 12 of them were published in her lifetime.

## A Yummy Creation
Ruth Wakefield, who—with her husband—owned the Toll House Inn near **Whitman**, is credited with inventing the chocolate chip cookie in the 1930s.

## A Peach of a Game
In 1891 **Springfield** physical education teacher James Naismith invented the game of basketball. The first game was played with a soccer ball using two peach baskets as goals.

## The Original Volley
The Volleyball Hall of Fame is in **Holyoke**—where the game was first invented by William G. Morgan in 1895. Morgan originally called his new game Mintonette.

## Lobster Lure
In 1808 Ebenezer Thorndike invented the lobster trap in the seaside town of **Swampscott**.

## A Smart Spot
In the Five College Area of Pioneer Valley (also called the Connecticut Valley), five institutions—the University of Massachusetts-Amherst, Hampshire College, Smith College, Mount Holyoke College, and Amherst College—are located within minutes of each other.

## A Sports Frenzy
Massachusetts is home to many professional sports teams including the Boston Celtics, Boston Bruins, New England Patriots, Boston Red Sox, and the New England Revolution. In addition, all the great college and university teams bring delight to their fans!

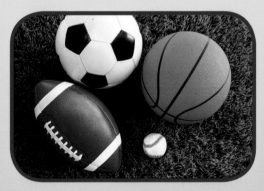

## A Famous Little Woman
Louisa May Alcott wrote her classic novel, *Little Women*, in **Concord** in 1868.

## Well Read Kids
In 1895, the Boston Pulbic Library was the first to open a special section for children.

# Find Out More

There are many great websites that can give you more information about the exciting things that are going on in the state of Massachusetts!

## State Websites

**The Official Website of Massachusetts**
www.mass.gov

**Massachusetts Department of Conservation and Recreation**
www.mass.gov/dcr

## Museums/Boston

**John F. Kennedy Presidential Library and Museum/Boston**
www.jfklibrary.org

**Massachusetts Museum of Contemporary Art**
www.massmoca.org

**Museum of African American History (Boston and Nantucket)**
www.afroammuseum.org

**Museum of Fine Arts**
www.mfa.org

## Cambridge

**Harvard Museum of Natural History**
www.hmnh.harvard.edu

## Gloucester

**Cape Ann Museum**
www.capeannhistoricalmuseum.org

## Lowell

**American Textile History Museum**
www.athm.org

## Plymouth

**Plimoth Plantation**
www.plimoth.org

## Springfield

**Basketball Hall of Fame**
www.hoophall.com

## Stockbridge

**Norman Rockwell Museum**
www.nrm.org

## Weston

**Spellman Museum of Stamps and Postal History**
www.spellman.org

## Aquarium and Zoos

**New England Aquarium (Boston)**
www.neaq.org

**Franklin Park Zoo (Boston)**
www.zoonewengland.org

**The Zoo in Forest Park and Education Center (Springfield)**
www.forestparkzoo.org

**Southwick's Zoo (Mendon)**
www.southwickszoo.com

**Stone Zoo (Stoneham)**
www.zoonewengland.org

# Massachusetts: At A Glance

State Capital: Boston

**Massachusetts Borders:** Rhode Island, Connecticut, New York, Vermont, New Hampshire, and the Atlantic Ocean

**Population:** 6,600,000

**Highest Point:** Mount Greylock—3,491 feet above sea level

**Lowest Point:** sea level at the Atlantic Ocean

**Some Major Cities:** Boston, Worcester, Springfield, Lowell, Cambridge, Brockton, New Bedford, Fall River, Quincy, Lynn

# Some Famous People from Massachusetts

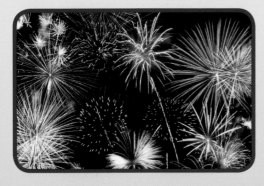

**Samuel Adams** (1722–1803) from Boston; was one of the Founding Fathers of the United States, Massachusetts delegate to the Continental Congress, and a leader of the American Revolution.

**Susan B. Anthony** (1820–1906) from West Grove; was a leader in the 19th-century women's rights movement.

**Clarissa "Clara" Barton** (1821–1912) from North Oxford; was a Civil War nurse and founder of the American Red Cross.

**William Edward Burghardt (W.E.B.) DuBois** (1868–1963) from Great Barrington; was a writer, historian, and civil rights activist.

**Benjamin Franklin** (1706–1790) from Boston; was one of the Founding Fathers of the United States (he signed both the Declaration of Independence and the Constitution), a printer, author, inventor, statesman, diplomat, and Postmaster General first of Philadelphia and later of the government of the Continental Congress.

**Winslow Homer** (1836–1910) from Boston; was a landscape painter considered to be one of the most important painters of 19th-century American art.

**John F. Kennedy** (1917–1963) from Brookline; was the 35th president of the United States.

**Sharon Christa McAuliffe** (1948–1986) from Boston; was a teacher and NASA astronaut who received the Congressional Space Medal of Honor.

**Barbara Walters** (born 1929) from Boston; is a broadcast journalist, TV host, and author.

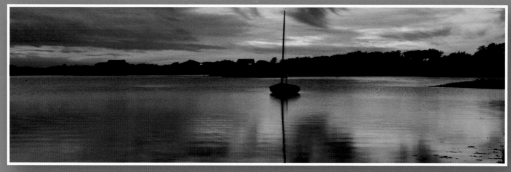

Sunset on Martha's Vineyard

## CREDITS

### Series Concept and Development
Kate Boehm Jerome

### Design
Steve Curtis Design, Inc. (www.SCDchicago.com); Roger Radtke, Todd Nossek

### Reviewers and Contributors
Content review: Julia J. Mize, Acting Education Specialist, Boston NHP; Contributing writers/editors: Terry B. Flohr, Stacey L. Klaman; Research and production: Judy Elgin Jensen; Copy editor: Mary L. Heaton

### Photography
Back Cover(a), 27f © Picsfive/Shutterstock; Back Cover(b), 2a © Jerry Moorman/iStockphoto; Back Cover(c), 10a © Marcio Jose Bastos Silva/Shutterstock; Back Cover(d), 3b © Ralph Roach/Shutterstock; Back Cover(e), 18-19 © Christian Delbert/Shutterstock; Cover(a), 2b © Chee-Onn Leong/Shutterstock; Cover(b), 26c By Justin Russell/From Wikipedia; Cover(c), 26b © Chas/Shutterstock; Cover(d) © Olga Miltsova/Shutterstock; Cover(e), 14-15 © Jennifer L. Harvey/Shutterstock; Cover(f) © Dave Newman/Shutterstock; 2-3, 32 © Jorge Salcedo/Shutterstock; 3a, 6-7, 7c © Denis Jr. Tangney/iStockphoto; 4-5 © Doug Lemke/Shutterstock; 5a, 20-21 © Ken Canning/iStockphoto; 5b © Mike Liu/Shutterstock; 7a © Jeff Schultes/Shutterstock; 7b © Bruce Barone/Shutterstock; 8-9 © Christopher Chan; 9a © Stephen Orsillo/iStockphoto; 9b Courtesy Massachusetts Department of Conservation and Recreation; 10-11 © Joy Brown/Shutterstock; 11a © Tim Gupta/iStockphoto; 11b © Lawrence Roberg/Shutterstock; 12-13 © 2010 Alex Tsai, flickr.com/alextsf; 13a © Israel Pabon/Shutterstock; 13b Sculpture and photo by Meredith Bergmann; 15a By Jeremy Clowe. © Norman Rockwell Museum. All rights reserved.; 15b Courtesy Spellman Museum of Stamps & Postal History; 16-17 By Greg Frechette; 17a, 28 © Marcos Carvalho/Shutterstock; 17b © Adrian LaRoque; 18a © Allan Pospisil/iStockphoto; 18b © Sam Chadwick/iStockphoto; 19a Courtesy Plimoth Plantation; 19b © marco mayer/Shutterstock; 21 © James DeBoer/Shutterstock; 22-23 © Kenneth Wiedemann/iStockphoto; 23a By Dann Blackwood/U.S. Geological Survey; 23b © Hywit Dimyadi/Shutterstock; 23c © John Wollwerth/Shutterstock; 24-25 Courtesy Eastern States Exposition; 25a © Pindyurin Vasily/Shutterstock; 25b © David P. Smith/Shutterstock; 26a © Steven J. Baskauf; 27a © Madlen/Shutterstock; 27b © Pakmor/Shutterstock; 27c © Lyle E. Doberstein/Shutterstock; 27d © Mike Neale/Shutterstock; 27e © catnap72/iStockphoto; 29a © VectorZilla/Shutterstock; 29b © Sandra Cunningham/Shutterstock; 31 © R. Gino Santa Maria/Shutterstock

### Illustration
Back Cover, 1, 4, 6 © Jennifer Thermes/Photodisc/Getty Images

ISBN 978-1-58973-019-9

Library of Congress Catalog Card Number: 2010935882

1 2 3 4 5 6 WPC 15 14 13 12 11 10

Published by Arcadia Publishing, Charleston, SC

For all general information contact Arcadia Publishing at:
Telephone   843-853-2070
Fax           843-853-0044
Email        sales@arcadiapublishing.com
For Customer Service and Orders:
Toll Free    1-888-313-2665

Visit us on the Internet at www.arcadiapublishing.com